Buying Property in Catalonia, Spain

A Step-by-Step Guide for Foreigners:
Real Costs, Mortgages, Taxes and What Can Go Wrong

Allen J. Woppert

Silo Publishing

Sitges, Barcelona, Spain

Allen J. Woppert/Silo Publishing
Sitges, Barcelona, Spain

Buying Property in Catalonia, Spain A Step-by-Step Guide for Foreigners—Real Costs, Mortgages, Taxes, and What Can Go Wrong / Allen J. Woppert

ISBN: 978-84-09-86589-5

Table of Contents

Introduction

Buying property in another country is rarely just a transaction.

It means navigating unfamiliar systems, learning new terminology, and making decisions with incomplete information—often while a great deal of money is at stake.

When my husband and I started the process of buying a property here in Sitges, one line from the classic film *The Wizard of Oz* kept coming to mind:

"We're not in Kansas anymore."

I have never actually lived in Kansas. I may have driven through it once. But the meaning was clear enough: we were in unfamiliar territory.

That is what this book is about.

I am not a lawyer, a real estate agent, or a mortgage specialist. I am someone who has gone through the process of buying property in Catalonia—twice—and who wished, at several points along the way, that there had been a clear, practical guide explaining what was happening and what questions we should be asking.

The information we needed was often available, but it was scattered, technical, or presented as if we already understood the system. We didn't. And if you are reading this book, you may be in a similar position.

You may be dreaming of a home in Catalonia. You may already be looking at properties. You may have found one and suddenly realized that the process is moving faster than expected.

This guide is designed to take some of the nervousness out of that process.

It will not replace professional advice. For legal, financial, or tax questions specific to your situation, you should consult the appropriate professional. But it should help you understand the structure of the purchase, the real costs involved, the documents and checks that matter, and the points at which decisions become binding.

In other words, it is meant to help you ask better questions.

Buying property may be one of the biggest financial decisions of your life. It is worth taking the time to understand what you are doing before you commit.

So let's get started.

Note: Updated resources, downloadable checklists, and additional information are available at www.allenjwoppert.com (Summer 2026)

1 What Makes Buying Property in Catalonia Different

Buying property in Catalonia is not complicated—but it is unfamiliar.

And unfamiliar is where expensive mistakes can happen.

If you've bought property before—in the UK, Germany, the US, or elsewhere—you may assume the process will feel broadly similar. In reality, several key aspects of buying in Catalonia work very differently, both legally and practically.

Understanding these differences early on can save you time, money, and a great deal of stress.

1. The Legal Structure Is Different

In many countries, the process of buying property is heavily standardized and closely guided. In Spain—and in Catalonia specifically—the structure is more flexible, but also less intuitive for outsiders.

For example:

- The notary does not represent your interests.
- Preliminary contracts are often private agreements between buyer and seller. (The final sale is, of course, public deed.)
- Legal protection depends largely on the lawyer you choose.

This means that responsibility is more directly in your hands than you might expect.

2. The "*Contrato de Arras*" Is a Critical Moment

One of the most important—and often misunderstood—steps is the *Contrato de Arras*—usually simply referred to as *Arras*—a private deposit contract signed before the final purchase.

You can think of it as a commitment backed by money. In the United States a similar concept is often referred to as "earnest money."

At this point:

- You typically pay around 10% of the purchase price. (The amount is negotiable. We paid slightly less.)
- If you withdraw, you usually lose that deposit. In some cases, the contract may include a clause allowing you to withdraw without penalty if financing cannot be obtained—but this must be explicitly agreed. (Note also that the burden of proof lies with the buyer: they must provide evidence that they made a serious attempt to procure financing, usually with several banks.) In the most common form—*Arras Penitenciales*—the seller must return double the deposit if they withdraw.

This is not just a formality. It is a legally binding commitment with real financial consequences. This is the time to do your due diligence (cf. Chapter 4).

Especially foreign buyers underestimate how significant this step is.

3. Costs Are Higher—and Less Obvious

The purchase price is only part of what you pay.

In Catalonia, transaction costs can typically add between 10% and 13% (or more) on top of the purchase price, including:

- Transfer tax (ITP)
- Notary and registry fees
- Legal costs
- Possible agent fees

What surprises many buyers is not just the level of these costs—but how little they are explained upfront.

4. Mortgages Work Differently

Spanish mortgages can be difficult to compare at first glance.

You'll encounter terms such as:

- TIN (nominal interest rate)
- TAE (true annual cost)
- *Bonificaciones* (conditional discounts)

What appears to be a competitive offer may depend on:

- taking out insurance
- using bank products
- meeting specific conditions

In practice, this means:

> the cheapest-looking mortgage is not always the cheapest overall.

5. The Role of the Estate Agent

In Catalonia, the estate agent typically:

- represents the seller, not the buyer
- is paid by the seller (usually from the sale price)
- may provide information—but is not responsible for protecting your interests

This is a key mindset shift for many buyers: You should assume that you are responsible for verifying everything independently.

6. Renovation Is Often Part of the Reality

Many properties—especially in desirable areas—require some level of renovation.

What is often underestimated:

- the true cost of work
- the time required for getting the necessary permits
- the complexity of dealing with contractors

A property that appears affordable may quickly become expensive once renovation is factored in.

7. Rules Around Rentals Are Strict

If you're planning to rent out the property, be aware that short-term rentals (such as Airbnb) are heavily regulated in Catalonia.

In many areas:

- a license is required
- new licenses may not be available
- transferring an existing license can be complex and time-consuming
- enforcement is active

This is particularly important if rental income is part of your plan.

Mid- and long-term rentals are generally possible, but local conditions should always be verified.

8. It's a Relationship-Driven Process

Finally, the process in Spain tends to be less transactional and more relationship-driven than in some other countries.

Communication may be:

- slower
- less formal
- occasionally unclear

This is not necessarily a problem—but it requires patience and careful follow-up.

None of these differences are inherently negative. But taken together, they mean one thing:

> You cannot rely on assumptions from your home country.

The more you understand how the system works in Catalonia, the more confidently—and safely—you can move through the process.

In the next chapter, we'll look at ***the full buying process*** *step by step, so you can see exactly how these elements fit together from the start.*

2 The Buying Process (Overview)

Before going into detail on individual steps, it helps to understand the overall structure of the process.

Buying property in Catalonia follows a logical sequence. While details may vary slightly from case to case, the key stages are broadly consistent.

Understanding this sequence will help you:

- know what to expect
- anticipate what comes next
- avoid being rushed into decisions

The Process at a Glance

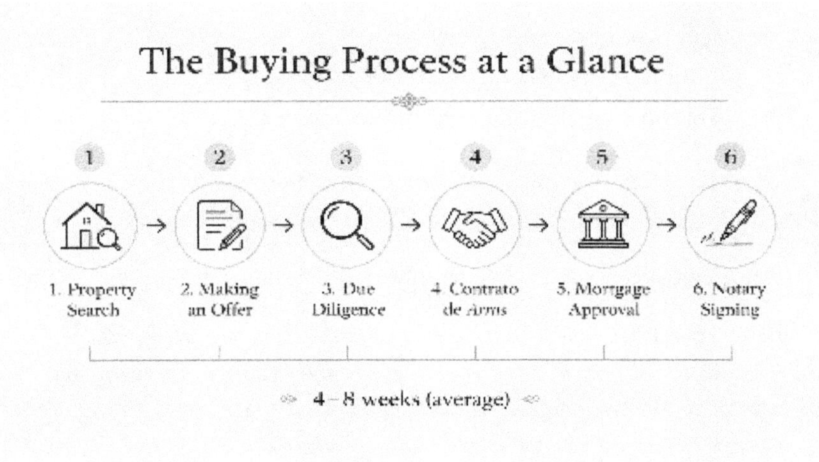

After this, there are a number of post-purchase steps, which we will cover later.

1. Property Search

This is where everything begins.

You may:

- browse online property portals. Here in Catalonia (and, I believe, the rest of Spain), the big ones are Idealista, Fotocasa and Habitaclia.
  Note that there's a lot of overlap between the portals. There may even be several listings of the same property on each of them, as estate agents/realtors do not usually have exclusive rights to represent a particular property.
- contact estate agents. By answering ads from the online portals, you'll have direct contact with different estate agents. Or you can simply walk into the offices of an estate agent and tell them what you're looking for. A good agent will keep records of these conversations and contact you if they have something you might be interested in.
- visit properties in person.

At this stage, it's easy to focus only on the property itself—location, price, condition. But it's equally important to start thinking ahead:

- Will you need a mortgage?
- Does the property require renovation?
- Are there any legal or structural concerns?

At this stage, you are gathering impressions—not making final decisions.

Before we move on, I'd like to share a few notes from our experience.

Before entering the process, but especially before talking to estate agents, we found it helpful to write down our criteria. We were able to narrow our search and save a lot of time by being clear about location, accessibility and size of the property we wanted. It also helped that we clarified our willingness to take on a renovation project.

When we first started to look for a place to buy, we kept our eyes open for signs hanging on balconies or the outside of buildings. Some were from estate agents, but some were from owners. "For sale by owner" sounded pretty good to us. But our experience was that the sellers had unrealistic expectations and none of the expert knowledge of the process an estate agent can provide. We eventually stopped contacting sellers directly and went with established realty professionals.

After months of scouting, we were seriously interested in three different properties: two apartments and one house. One of the apartments was move-in ready; the other required a bit of work. The house was a clear fixer-upper.

We looked at the places on our short list two, three or more times. The move-in ready flat turned out to be less interesting on the second visit due to its location. It was, however, beautifully appointed, and the estate agent was happy to give us the name of the interior designer/ architect who had designed it. We ended up using her services for the house we finally bought.

The not-quite ready apartment seemed less attractive the second time, but the fixer-upper tugged at our heartstrings again on the second visit. We went two more times with architects who gave us an idea what work would be necessary to turn the house into our dream home and what we were getting into financially. We paid one of the architects to do a thorough home inspection, which set us back about €700.

2. Making an Offer

Once you've found a property you're interested in, you can make an offer, usually through the estate agent.

Offers can be:

- verbal (initial indication)
- written (more formal and often preferred)

Negotiation is common, but not always dramatic. In some cases, properties sell quickly and at or near the asking price.

If your offer is accepted, the property is usually taken off the market—at least informally. The estate agent may draw up an informal contract, and a small deposit may be required.

At this point, neither your offer nor its acceptance is legally binding, but you should definitely read the deposit contract carefully to be sure.

Once things have progressed this far, the purchase can move quite quickly.

3. Due Diligence

Due diligence (dealt with in Chapter 4) involves verifying that:

- the property is legally registered and free of unexpected charges
- the seller is in fact the owner and entitled to sell the property
- taxes and community fees (if applicable) are up to date
- the property complies with planning and usage regulations

As the signing of the *Contrato de Arras* approaches, you need to start doing your due diligence. Although some checks will continue afterward, the more you can verify in advance, the lower your risk.

4. The *Contrato de Arras*

The *Contrato de Arras* is a private contract between buyer and seller that:

- confirms the agreed price
- sets a timeline for completion of the sale (usually known as "closing" in the USA)
- requires a deposit (typically around 10%)

Why this step is critical

From this point on:

- the property is taken off the market
- both parties are committed
- there are financial consequences if either side withdraws

5. Financing and Mortgage Approval

If you require a mortgage, this stage runs alongside—or immediately after—the *Arras* contract.

This typically involves:

- submitting documentation to one or more banks
- obtaining a property evaluation (*tasación*)
- receiving a formal offer (FEIN)

Important

Mortgage approval is not guaranteed.

> You should have a clear understanding of your financing position before committing to *Arras*, or ensure that appropriate conditions are included in the *Arras* contract.

Again, I'd like to share our experience.

We had been customers of one bank for more than ten years and had always been happy with their service. We considered it "our bank." So it seemed obvious to us that we would finance our house with them. What a mistake that was!

The financing department was exceedingly unprofessional. Instead of providing us with a list of documents we would need to produce, this step was done piecemeal. It seemed that every few days there would be a call, email or text message from the bank asking for some new document.

We eventually decided we needed to look at other banks, and we solicited offers from three more. I guess we'd been pretty naïve, but we were shocked at the differences between the offers.

In the end, we did get two attractive offers. They looked nearly identical to us, but when our lawyer reviewed the contracts, it turned out there was a clear winner. AI confirmed what the lawyer had recommended and even found a few things the lawyer had missed. (To be fair, the attorney also found a few items the AI didn't.)

Another big surprise for us was that we had to see a notary and take a sort of test to show that we understood the mortgage contract in all its essential details. This pre-signing meeting is mandatory (acta previa).

6. Completion at the Notary

The final step is the signing of the public deed (*escritura pública*) at the notary. It is worth mentioning that, as the buyer, you have the final say as to which notary is used. We let the estate agent choose.

At this stage:

- the deed is signed
- the remaining purchase price is paid
- ownership is formally transferred
- the transaction becomes legally binding and complete

The notary reads the purchase contract out loud (or gives an oral summary), confirms identities, and ensures that the legal requirements are met.

Once the contract is signed, you are officially the owner of the property.

Timing: How Long Does It Take?

From accepted offer to final signing, the process typically takes from 4 to 8 weeks.

This depends on:

- how quickly the *Arras* contract is prepared
- whether a mortgage is involved
- how organized all parties are

Delays are not unusual—but they are usually manageable if anticipated.

Where Delays Can Occur

While the process is structured, delays are not uncommon.

Typical causes include:

- incomplete documentation
- issues uncovered during due diligence
- mortgage approval taking longer than expected
- coordination between multiple parties

The process is structured—but not necessarily sequential.

Understanding this helps you stay flexible without losing control.

Why This Overview Matters

Many of the problems buyers encounter come from:

- not understanding when decisions become binding
- assuming there is more time than there actually is
- reacting to events rather than anticipating them

With a clear overview of the process, you are better able to:

- plan ahead
- ask the right questions
- and move forward with confidence

In the next chapter, we'll look in detail at one of the most important—and often underestimated—aspects of buying property in Catalonia: ***the real costs*** *involved in buying property in Catalonia.*

3 The Real Costs

One of the most common mistakes buyers make is focusing almost entirely on the purchase price.

In reality, the purchase price is only part of the financial picture.

By the time the transaction is complete, the total cost of buying a property is typically significantly higher than the advertised price once taxes, legal fees, and related expenses are included.

Understanding these costs early is essential—not only for budgeting, but also for determining whether a purchase is realistically affordable.

The Rule of Thumb

As a general guideline, buyers should expect total acquisition costs to add approximately:

> 10%–13% (or more) on top of the purchase price.

The exact figure depends on:

- the type of property
- whether a mortgage is involved
- the buyer's tax situation
- and the services used during the transaction

The Main Costs

The most common purchase-related costs include:

- Transfer tax (ITP)
- Notary fees
- Land Registry fees
- Legal fees
- Mortgage-related costs
- Possible renovation or setup expenses

Some of these are unavoidable. Others depend on the choices you make during the process.

Example Cost Breakdown: Typical Purchase Costs in Catalonia

Cost Type	What It Covers	€250,000 Property	€400,000 Property	Notes
Purchase Price	Agreed price with seller	€250,000	€400,000	Base price only
Transfer Tax (ITP)	Property transfer tax (typically 10% for most buyers in Catalonia)	€25,000	€40,000	Usually the largest additional cost
Notary Fees	Signing of public deed (*escritura pública*)	€600 to €1,000	€800 to €1,200	Depends on property value and transaction complexity
Land Registry	Registration of ownership	€400 to €700	€600 to €900	Paid after completion/closing
Legal Fees	Lawyer review and transaction support	~€2,500	~€4,000	Often around 1% (+ IVA/VAT)

Cost Type	What It Covers	€250,000 Property	€400,000 Property	Notes
Mortgage Valuation	Property valuation required for mortgage	€300–€600	€300 to €600	Normally paid by buyer; actual cost varies
Total Estimated Cost	Purchase price + all above costs	~€279,800	~€446,700	Approximate overall total

These figures are indicative only and will vary depending on the property, financing structure, and professional services used.

1. Transfer Tax (ITP)

For most resale properties in Catalonia, buyers pay:
ITP (Impuesto de Transmisiones Patrimoniales).

This is generally:

- the largest additional cost
- paid by the buyer
- due shortly after completion

The applicable rate can change over time and may vary depending on:

- the value of the property
- the buyer's circumstances
- current regional tax rules

Important: the tax may not be calculated on the purchase price.

The taxable value of the property is not necessarily the price you pay. If the property has an official *valor de referencia* (reference value), ITP is generally calculated using the highest of:

- the *valor de referencia*
- the value declared in the transaction
- the agreed purchase price

If there is no applicable *valor de referencia*, different valuation rules apply.

This matters because the taxable value can be higher than the purchase price. Before committing to a property, check both the current ITP rate **and the value on which the tax will be calculated**.

> Always verify the current rules before purchasing.

2. Notary Fees

The notary formalizes the transaction and prepares the public deed (*escritura pública*).

Notary fees are:

- regulated
- generally predictable
- based partly on the property value and documentation involved

Compared with taxes, these costs are relatively modest—but still important to budget for.

3. Land Registry Fees

After completion, the property must be registered in your name at the *Registro de la Propiedad.*

These fees cover the formal registration of ownership and related administrative procedures.

4. Legal Fees

Although using a lawyer is not legally required, it is strongly recommended—especially for foreign buyers.

Legal fees typically cover:

- contract review

- due diligence
- communication with the seller and agents
- coordination of the transaction

A practical point

Not all lawyers are created equal. The cheapest lawyer isn't always the best value.

A good lawyer may save you significantly more than their fee by identifying problems early.

5. Mortgage-Related Costs (if applicable)

If you are taking out a mortgage (*hipoteca*), there may still be additional costs for you as the borrower. Under current Spanish mortgage law, the borrower normally pays for the property valuation (*tasación*), while the lender bears the notary, Land Registry, tax and *gestoría* costs associated with formalizing the mortgage.

Other costs to the borrower may include:

- property valuation (*tasación*)
- an opening fee, if the lender charges one
- insurance or other linked products you choose or are required to arrange under the mortgage terms

Important

What appears to be a low-interest mortgage may involve:

- expensive insurance
- account requirements
- or other linked products

> Always evaluate the total cost—not just the headline interest rate.

6. Renovation and Setup Costs

Many buyers focus heavily on acquisition costs while underestimating what comes afterward.

Additional expenses may include:

- renovation work
- furniture and appliances
- utility deposits and setup
- painting and repairs

A common mistake

A property may appear affordable until renovation and setup costs are added.

This is particularly common with:

- older apartments
- rural properties
- properties marketed as "full of potential"

Costs That Surprise Foreign Buyers

Foreign buyers are often surprised by:

- how high transfer taxes are
- how quickly costs accumulate
- the amount of cash required upfront

This is especially important because Spanish banks typically do not finance purchase costs separately.

Buyers must usually cover these separately using their own funds.

Cash Flow Matters

Many buyers focus primarily on monthly mortgage payments.

But the more immediate challenge is often having enough cash available to complete the purchase.

In practice, buyers may need funds for:

- deposit (*Arras*)
- taxes
- legal costs
- notary and registry fees
- mortgage-related expenses
- renovations or repairs

Before committing to a property:

- calculate all acquisition costs realistically
- include contingency funds
- avoid assuming everything will go exactly to plan

A useful rule

> If your budget only works under perfect conditions, your budget is probably too tight.

Now that you understand the full cost picture, the next step is to ensure that the property you're buying is legally and structurally sound. In the next chapter, we'll look at the **due diligence** *checks you should carry out before committing to the purchase.*

4 Due Diligence: What To Check Before You Commit

Buying property in Catalonia is not simply about finding the right property and agreeing on a price.

Before you commit—especially before signing the *Contrato de Arras*—you need to answer a more important question:
Is this property legally, financially, and practically sound?

This process is known as due diligence.

It is where many problems are either discovered—or missed.

And once you move past the *Arras* stage, your ability to walk away becomes limited and often expensive.

Why Due Diligence Matters

In some countries, many checks are built into the process.

In Spain, responsibility is more decentralized.

This means:

- no single party is automatically checking everything for you
- different aspects (legal, technical, financial) are handled separately
- gaps can occur if no one is actively coordinating the process

In practice, this makes due diligence one of the most important stages of the entire purchase.

When Should These Checks Be Done?

Ideally, before signing the *Contrato de Arras*

In reality:

- some checks are done before signing the *Contrato de Arras*
- others continue between *Arras* and final signing

But the key point is:

> The more you verify before committing, the lower your risk.

The Key Checks Explained

1. Ownership and Legal Status

The first step is to confirm:

- who legally owns the property
- whether the seller has the right to sell
- whether there are any charges, debts, or encumbrances

This information is typically obtained through a *Nota Simple*. It can be requested through the local office of the *Registro de la Propiedad* or online via the official *Colegio de Registradores* website (www.registradores.org).

You need to ensure:

- you are buying from the correct legal owner
- there are no unexpected liabilities attached to the property

2. Debts and Charges

In addition to registry checks, you should confirm:

- no outstanding property tax (IBI)
- no unpaid community fees

- no utility debts

Certain obligations—particularly community debts—may remain attached to the property rather than the previous owner. In other words, you buy the obligations along with the property.

3. Cadastral vs. Actual Property

In Spain, it is not uncommon for:

- the registered size
- the cadastral record
- and the physical reality of a property

to differ.

You (or your lawyer) should verify:

- square meters
- layout
- existence of terraces, extensions, or storage areas

Unregistered elements can:

- create legal issues
- affect resale value
- require (possibly expensive) correction later

4. Urban Planning and Legal Compliance

This is one of the most important—and most overlooked—areas.

You need to confirm that:

- the property is legally built
- all parts are compliant with local planning regulations
- there are no pending sanctions or demolition risks

This confirmation is especially important for:

- older properties
- rural homes
- properties with visible modifications

5. The Community of Owners (Apartments and Shared Developments)

If the property is part of a shared building or development (e.g. a "gated community"), check:

- current community fees
- outstanding debts
- planned major works

Why this matters

You may inherit:

- unpaid contributions
- significant future costs (e.g. façade or roof repairs, lift installation)

6. Technical Condition of the Property

Legal checks are only part of the picture.

You should also assess:

- structural condition
- electrical and plumbing systems
- damp or insulation issues

This can be done through:

- your own inspection
- or a professional survey (recommended for older properties)

7. Renovations and Permits

If the property has been modified, check:

- whether permits were obtained
- whether changes were properly registered

Unlicensed work can:

- lead to fines
- complicate resale
- require costly regularization

From our experience: The little house we decided to buy had a small rooftop addition that had never been permitted. Fortunately, the structure had appeared in aerial photographs for many years and had effectively become part of the cadastral record—"grandfathered in," so to speak. Lesson: Find out as much about your property's history as you can.

8. Mortgage Feasibility (If Applicable)

If you need financing, you should have the following before signing the *Contrato de Arras*:

- a realistic understanding of your borrowing capacity
- ideally, pre-approval from a bank

> If your mortgage is not approved, you may still be bound by the *Arras* contract.

9. Rental and Usage Restrictions

If you plan to rent out the property short term, check:

- whether short-term rental licenses are required
- whether they are available in that area
- whether existing licenses are transferable
- building-level restrictions (community rules)

In many parts of Catalonia, short-term rentals are tightly controlled or restricted.

Where Problems Usually Arise

In practice, issues tend to come from:

- checks started too late
- incomplete or rushed legal review
- assumptions based on verbal assurances
- relying too heavily on agents

> If something is unclear before signing the *Contrato de Arras*, it becomes your problem after signing it.

Due Diligence Checklist (Before Signing the *Contrato de Arras*)

Area to Check	What to Verify	Document / Information	Where to Request It	Notes
Ownership & Registry	Legal owner Right to sell Charges Correct description	*Nota Simple*	*Registro de la Propiedad*	usually valid for ~3 months
Property Tax (IBI)	No outstanding IBI All years paid	IBI receipt + debt certificate	*Ayuntamiento – Departamento de Gestión Tributaria / Recaudación*	Ask for *certificado de estar al corriente de pago del IBI.*
Cadastral Information	Size Boundaries Structures	*Cédula Catastral / Consulta Descriptiva y Gráfica*	*Dirección General del Catastro*	online: sedecatastro.gob.es

Area to Check	What to Verify	Document / Information	Where to Request It	Notes
Urban Planning & Legal Status	Legal build Zoning No sanctions	*Certificado Urbanístico* (if available)	*Ayuntamiento – Área de Urbanismo / Planeamiento*	critical for older or modified properties
Community of Owners (if applicable)	No debts, fees, planned works	*Certificado de deuda cero*	*Administrador de Fincas / Presidente de la Comunidad*	required for apartments
Utilities & Debts	No unpaid electricity, water, gas	Latest bills / confirmations	utility providers (*Compañía Eléctrica, Agua, Gas*)	Ask seller for proof.
Renovations & Permits	Works permitted and registered	*Licencia de Obras* + *Certificado de Habitabilidad*	*Ayuntamiento – Licencias de Obras*	unlicensed work = risk
Financing (if applicable)	Mortgage feasibility	*Preaprobación hipotecaria*	Banco / *Entidad financiera*	Do before *Arras*.
Rental Restrictions	Airbnb rules, community rules	*Estatutos* / local regulations	*Ayuntamiento* + *Comunidad de Propietarios*	licenses often restricted

Due diligence does not make the process slower. It makes it safer. And in most cases, problems are not hidden—they are simply not checked.

> It is impossible to eliminate all risk from your home purchase. But you need to eliminate whatever risk you can, preferably before committing to the purchase. And it's good to understand what you are buying, as fully and clearly as possible.

Now that you know what needs to be checked, the next step is to understand how to navigate one of the most important—and most binding—moments in the process, the ***Contrato de Arras*****.**

5 The *Contrato de Arras*

At a certain point in the buying process, the transaction changes from exploratory to binding.

In Catalonia, that moment is the signing of the *Contrato de Arras*.

What Is the *Contrato de Arras*?

The *Contrato de Arras* is a private contract between buyer and seller that sets out:

- the agreed purchase price
- the parties involved
- the timeline for completion of the sale
- the deposit to be paid

In most cases, the deposit is around 10% of the purchase price.

What makes this contract different

Unlike an informal agreement, the *Arras* contract is legally binding.

It is more than a reservation agreement. It is a commitment with financial consequences.

Why This Stage Matters So Much

Up to this point, you can walk away relatively easily.

After signing the *Contrato de Arras*:

- your flexibility is limited
- your financial exposure increases
- your decisions become binding

This is why everything in the previous chapter—due diligence—is so important.

What Happens When You Sign

Immediately after signing:

- you pay the agreed deposit (typically ~10%)
- the property is formally taken off the market
- a completion/closing date is set (usually a few weeks later)

From this point on, both the buyer and the seller are committed to completing the transaction.

The Key Rule: What Happens If Someone Walks Away

This is the most important aspect of the *Contrato de Arras*.

> If the buyer withdraws:
> you typically lose your deposit.
>
> If the seller withdraws:
> they must usually return double the deposit.

This structure is designed to:

- create commitment on both sides
- discourage last-minute changes

Types of *Arras* Contracts (Briefly)

There are different legal forms of *Arras*, but the most common in practice is:

Arras penitenciales

This is the version that includes:

- loss of deposit (buyer)
- double repayment (seller)

In most cases, this is the default—but it should not be assumed. Your lawyer should confirm the exact type used.

What Should Be Included in the Contract

A properly drafted *Contrato de Arras* should clearly state:

- full details of buyer and seller
- precise identification of the property
- agreed purchase price
- deposit amount
- deadline for completion of sale
- distribution of costs
- conditions (if any)

Conditions: Can You Protect Yourself?

In some cases, the contract can include conditions.

For example:

- subject to mortgage approval
- subject to satisfactory legal checks

Important reality

In competitive markets:

- sellers prefer unconditional offers
- adding conditions may weaken your position

This creates a balance between:

- protecting yourself
- securing the property

Common Risks at the *Arras* Stage

Problems at this stage often arise from:

- signing too quickly under pressure
- incomplete due diligence
- unclear financing
- misunderstanding contract terms

A typical mistake

A buyer signs *Arras* assuming "Everything will work out."

But:

- the mortgage is delayed or denied
- an issue is discovered later

At that point, the deposit is at risk.

Timing: How Long Between *Arras* and Completion?

Typically **between four and eight weeks**.

During this period:

- final checks are completed
- mortgage is finalized
- documents are prepared

Who Prepares the Contract?

The *Arras* contract is often:

- drafted by the estate agent
- or provided by the seller

> Your lawyer should review (and ideally revise) the contract before signing.

The Role of the Notary (At This Stage)

At the *Arras* stage, the notary is not yet involved.

This is a private agreement, which makes it no less binding.

That means:

- fewer safeguards
- more reliance on your own preparation

In our case, the *Arras* was drafted by the estate agent and signed in their office.

A Practical Approach

Before signing the *Contrato de Arras*, you should be confident that:

- due diligence checks are complete or well advanced
- financing is realistic and secure
- the contract has been reviewed by your lawyer

- you fully understand the consequences

> The *Contrato de Arras* is the point where interest becomes obligation.

The significance of the *Contrato de Arras* becomes clearer when you compare the situation before and after signing:

Before vs After the *Contrato de Arras*

	Before *Arras*	**After *Arras***
Commitment level	Low	High
Ability to walk away	✓□ Easy	✕ Limited
Financial risk	Minimal	⚠□ Deposit at risk
Deposit paid	✕ No	✓□ ~10% paid
Property status	Still negotiable	Off the market
Due diligence	In progress	Should be substantially complete
Financing	Exploratory	Must be secured
Pressure level	Moderate	High

Once the *Contrato de Arras* is signed, the focus shifts to completing the transaction.

In the next chapter, we'll look at ***mortgages and financing in Spain****—how they work, and how to evaluate them properly.*

6 Mortgages in Spain

For many buyers, the mortgage is the most complex part of the entire process.

Not because it is inherently complicated—but because it is presented in a way that can be difficult to interpret.

Different banks use different terminology, conditions, and structures. What looks like a good offer at first glance may not be the best option in practice.

The purpose of this chapter is simple: to help you understand how Spanish mortgages actually work—and how to evaluate them with confidence.

The Basic Structure

Most mortgages in Spain fall into one of three categories:

- Fixed rate → interest remains the same for the entire term
- Variable rate → based on Euribor + margin
- Mixed rate → fixed for an initial period, then variable

Euribor (Euro Interbank Offered Rate) is the benchmark interest rate commonly used for variable-rate mortgages across the Eurozone. It is the average interest rate at which European banks lend money to each other.

What most buyers choose

In recent years, many buyers—especially foreign buyers—prefer fixed-rate mortgages because they:

- provide certainty
- are easier to plan around
- avoid exposure to interest rate changes

TIN vs. TAE – What Do They Actually Mean?

This is where confusion usually begins. The two terms refer to different ways of looking at interest.

TIN (*Tipo de Interés Nominal*)

- the headline interest rate
- used to calculate monthly payments

This is what most people focus on—but it does not tell the full story.

TAE (*Tasa Anual Equivalente*)

- the true annual cost of the mortgage
- includes additional costs and conditions

This is the number you should use to compare offers.

> A lower TIN does not necessarily mean a cheaper mortgage.

Bonificaciones – Discounts That Can Cost You Money

Many Spanish banks offer *bonificaciones* (interest rate discounts). These are typically conditional on:

- taking out life insurance
- taking out home insurance

- using the bank account actively
- paying your salary or pension into the account

These products:

- reduce your interest rate
- but increase your overall cost

What you should ask:

- What is the rate without *bonificaciones*?
- What is the total cost of the required products?
- Do I have to buy the insurance policies from the bank, or can I purchase cheaper but equivalent policies elsewhere?

Only when you have answered these questions can you compare offers properly.

What Banks Look For

When assessing your application, banks typically consider:

- income and stability
- existing debts
- age
- nationality and residency status
- type of employment (employed vs self-employed)

Loan-to-Value (LTV): How Much the Bank Will Lend

When a bank evaluates your mortgage application, one of the key numbers it uses is:

Loan-to-Value (LTV)

What does LTV mean? In Spanish this is referred to as *Ratio or Relación préstamo–valor*, although lenders often use the English abbreviation "LTV".

LTV is the percentage of the property's value that the bank is willing to finance.

It is usually calculated as:

Loan amount ÷ property value (or valuation) = LTV

Example:

- Property price: €300,000
- Bank lends up to 80% of value = €240,000

→ LTV = €240,000 ÷ €300,000 = **80%**

Why LTV matters

LTV determines how much cash you need upfront because the bank will not normally finance 100% of the purchase.

Typical LTV ranges required:

- Residents may typically borrow up to ~80%
- Non-residents: typically 60–70%

The LTV is usually calculated based on the **lower** of:

- the purchase price
- the bank's valuation (*tasación*) of the property

Example:

- Purchase price: €300,000
- Valuation: €280,000

→ 80% of €280,000 = €224,000 . **not** €240,000 (80% of €300,000); **€224,000 is the maximum amount the bank will lend.**

Note that an LTV under the limit is no guarantee that your loan will be approved. The bank will also evaluate your ability to manage the monthly payments.

If the valuation comes in lower than expected, you will need to provide more cash.

As a rule of thumb, a **resident** buyer will need 30%–40% of the purchase price in cash to pay:

- the part not covered by the mortgage
- taxes (e.g. ITP)
- fees and other costs

In the case of a **non-resident** , the amount increases to 40%–50% cash needed for the purchase.

The table shows figures for a house purchase for €300,000 with a valuation of €280,000.

	Resident (80% LTV)	Non-resident (70% LTV)	Non-resident (60% LTV)
Purchase price	€300,000	€300,000	€300,000
Property valuation	€280,000	€280,000	€280,000
Maximum mortgage amount	€224,000	€196,000	€168,000
Difference to purchase price	€76,000	€104,000	€132,000
Costs (~10% purchase price)	€30,000	€30,000	€30,000
Total cash needed	€106,000 (35% of purchase price)	€134,000 ((45% of purchase price)	€162,000 (54% of purchase price)

A Practical Insight

Many buyers focus on the question, "Can I afford the monthly payment?"

But the first question should be, "Do I have enough cash to complete the purchase?"

Your mortgage determines your monthly cost. Your LTV determines whether you can buy the property at all.

The Mortgage Process (Simplified)

Once you decide to proceed with a bank:

- Initial assessment / simulation
- Document submission
- Property valuation (*tasación*)
- Formal offer issued (FEIN)
- Cooling-off period
- Signing at the notary

The FEIN – Your Official Offer

The FEIN (*Ficha Europea de Información Normalizada*) is the legally binding mortgage offer.

It includes:

- interest rate
- monthly payments
- conditions
- total cost

Once the FEIN has been issued:

- conditions cannot be changed by the bank
- you have time to review before signing (usually 10 to 14 days)

If you fail to sign the FEIN within the time allotted, the offer expires. In turbulent times, the offer could be radically different after the deadline.

In our case, we had a competitive offer (FEIN) that was expiring, but we hadn't received the definitive offer from another bank that had sounded quite promising. We felt pressured to sign with the first bank before the offer expired. We did sign, and two days later the second bank came through with a considerably better offer.

Initially, we believed signing the first FEIN had locked us into that mortgage. Fortunately, we later confirmed that this was not the case: while the FEIN is binding for the bank, the buyer is generally not committed until the final mortgage and purchase documents are signed.

Documents Banks Typically Require

This is where preparation can save significant time.

Different banks may vary—but most will ask for a similar set of documents. Give the banks only the documents they ask for; unnecessary documentation can slow the review process.

Checklist: Commonly required documents

- Personal Identification
  - Passport or ID
  - NIE (*Número de Identidad de Extranjero*) or TIE (*Tarjeta de Identidad de Extranjero*)
  - Proof of address (*Certificado/Volante de Empadronamiento*, available from your local town hall or online)
- Income & employment
- If employed:
  - Recent pay slips (usually last 3 months)
  - Employment contract
  - Employer certificate (sometimes)
- If self-employed or retired:
  - Tax returns (*Declaración de la renta*, last 1–3 years)
  - Income statements
  - Accountant certification (in some cases)
- Financial information
  - Bank statements (typically last 3–6 months)
  - Details of existing loans or liabilities
  - Credit commitments (including credit card debt)
- Tax Documentation
  - Latest tax return
  - Proof that taxes are paid up to date (*Certificado al Corriente AEAT*)

  - Proof of income declarations
  - Proof of tax residency in Spain (*Residencia fiscal en España*)
- Property-Related Documents
  - Reservation agreement (if applicable)
  - Property details (*Nota simple*)
  - Valuation report (*tasación*, usually arranged by bank at buyer's expense). Some buyers choose to obtain an independent valuation early in the process to avoid paying for multiple valuations with different banks. Note, however, that not all banks will accept external reports.

Additional Documents (Sometimes Required)

- Proof of savings
- Marital status documentation (including any contract specifying how assets would be distributed in the event the union is dissolved)
- Certified translation of foreign documents
- Credit report from home country
- Work history (*Vida laboral*)

Common Pitfalls

Most problems with mortgages come from:

- incomplete documentation
- underestimating timelines
- misunderstanding *bonificaciones*
- comparing offers based only on TIN

A Practical Approach

To avoid issues:

- prepare documents early
- speak to more than one bank
- compare using TAE and total cost shown in the FEIN
- clarify all conditions

If you don't understand the conditions of your mortgage, you don't yet understand the cost of your property.

Understanding it properly gives you:

- control
- clarity
- confidence

With your financing in place, the final step is to complete the purchase. In the next chapter, we'll walk through the ***notary signing*** *and what happens on completion/closing day.*

7 Completion: Signing at the Notary

After weeks of preparation—searching, negotiating, checking, and arranging financing—you reach the final step, the signing at the notary.

This is the moment when the purchase becomes legally complete, and ownership of the property is transferred to you.

What Is the Notary's Role?

In Spain, the notary (*notario*) is a public official responsible for:

- verifying the identity of the parties
- ensuring the legality of the transaction
- reading and formalizing the deed

Important

The notary:

- is independent
- does not represent you or the seller
- ensures that the transaction complies with the law

What Is Signed?

At the notary, you sign the *Escritura Pública de Compraventa*, (the public deed of sale).

This document includes:

- identification of buyer and seller
- full description of the property
- agreed purchase price
- confirmation of payment
- statements regarding taxes and debts

Who Is Present?

Typically, the following people attend:

- buyer
- seller
- notary
- bank representative (if there is a mortgage)
- sometimes lawyers or agents

Before the Appointment

In the days leading up to the signing:

- final figures are confirmed
- funds are prepared
- documents are reviewed

If you have a mortgage:

You will also have:

- reviewed and signed the mortgage documentation in advance
- completed a mandatory meeting with the notary, during which the notary verifies that you understand the mortgage terms and conditions (cooling-off requirement)

How Payment Is Made

Payment is made:

- via banker's cheque (*cheque bancario*)
- or by bank transfer

If payment is by banker's cheque, the cheque(s) will be prepared in advance and handed over at the notary: one from the bank for the mortgage amount and one from you for the remainder of the purchase price (minus any amounts already paid at the *Arras*, for example).

If bank transfer is arranged, the bank representative will transfer the purchase price—including the mortgage amount—to the seller at the end of the notary session. If this is the path chosen, you will have to discuss with your bank how much you need to have in your account.

What to Bring to the Notary

Before attending the notary appointment, make sure you have all required documents and items ready.

What to Bring	Specifically	Notes
Identification	• Valid passport or national ID • NIE (*Número de Identidad de Extranjero*) or TIE (*Tarjeta de Identidad de Extranjero*)	Required to sign and register the property

What to Bring	Specifically	Notes

Payment	• Banker's cheque(s) (*cheque bancario*) for the purchase price
	• Additional cheques for:
	  o Taxes
	  o Notary fees
	  o Registry fees
		The cheque for the purchase price is prepared by your bank in advance.
		
		Additional cheques may be prepared by your bank, or the amounts may be paid after the notary appointment. Discuss this with the estate agent, bank or notary.
		
		Alternatively, the bank representative may transfer funds at the end of the signing.

Mortgage Documentation	• Confirmation of mortgage approval • Bank representative present • Proof of prior notary meeting (cooling-off requirement=	
Final Contract Documents	• Copy of the *Contrato de Arras* • Draft of the *Escritura Pública* (if provided in advance)	Review beforehand to avoid surprises.
Proof of Payments Already Made	• Deposit payment confirmation • Any prior transfer receipts	

What to Bring	Specifically	Notes
Property-Related Documents	• Latest IBI receipt (*Impuesto sobre Bienes Inmuebles*) • Energy certificate (*Certificado de Eficiencia Energética*) • Certificate of no community debts (*Certificado de deuda cero*)	These documents are typically provided by the seller, but worth verifying
Practical Items	• Means of communication with your lawyer or advisor • Notebook or phone for notes • Time buffer (avoid rushing the appointment)	

Remember: The notary appointment should be a formality—not a moment for surprises.

What Happens During the Signing

The process is structured but usually straightforward:

1. The notary confirms identities
2. The deed is read (or summarized) out loud by the notary
3. Any final questions are addressed
4. Documents are signed
5. Payments and keys are exchanged

Time required:

typically **30 to 60 minutes**

What You Should Pay Attention To

Even though this is the final step, it is still important to:

- ensure names and details are correct
- confirm the price and payment structure
- check any last-minute clauses

> If something is unclear, ask before signing.

What Happens Immediately After

Once the deed is signed, you are legally the owner.

You will typically:

- receive the keys
- take possession of the property

Registration and Taxes

After the signing:

- the deed is sent to the Land Registry (*Registro de la Propiedad*)
- the purchase is formally registered

You (or your bank, lawyer or *gestor*) will also:

- pay the relevant taxes (e.g. ITP)

Steps After Completion

Shortly after the purchase, you should:

- transfer utilities into your name
- inform the community of owners (if applicable)

- arrange insurance
- update your address where necessary

Common Misconceptions

"The notary is there to protect me."

Wrong. The notary ensures the legality of the transaction—but:

- does not replace your lawyer
- does not verify everything independently

"Everything is checked at the end"

By the time you reach the notary, most decisions have already been made.

This is why the preparation in earlier chapters is so important.

For many buyers, the notary appointment feels formal—or even intimidating.

In reality, it is the natural conclusion of a process you have already prepared for.

If everything has been handled properly:

- there should be no surprises
- the process should be smooth
- and the outcome is clear

A Simple Way to Think About It

The notary signing does not create the deal—it confirms it.

Why This Moment Matters

Beyond the legal formalities, this is also a personal milestone.

After navigating an unfamiliar system, making decisions, and managing risks, you now own a property in Catalonia.

With the purchase complete, the focus shifts from buying to owning.

In the next chapter, we'll look at ***what happens after the purchase****—ongoing costs, responsibilities, and practical considerations.*

8 After the Purchase

Signing at the notary may feel like the end of the process.

In reality, it is the beginning of a new phase.

Once you own the property, there are a number of practical, legal, and financial steps to complete—some immediately, others over time.

Understanding these early will help you settle in smoothly and avoid unnecessary complications.

What Happens Immediately After Signing

Once the deed has been signed:

- you receive the keys
- ownership is transferred
- the transaction is legally complete

However, several administrative steps still need to follow.

In most cases, your lawyer or gestor will handle some of these—but it is important to understand what is happening in your name.

1. Payment of Taxes

Shortly after the purchase, you must pay the applicable tax.

For most resale properties in Catalonia:

ITP (*Impuesto de Transmisiones Patrimoniales*)

Payment and filing are generally due within one month of the date of the purchase. In our case the bank dealt with the formalities.

Important:

Failure to pay on time may result in:

- penalties
- interest charges

IBI (annual property tax)

The seller normally has paid the IBI for the entire year of the sale. (The owner on 1st January is liable for the payment.) Proof of payment is then submitted to the buyer—most often through the estate agent—so that the buyer can reimburse the seller on a prorated basis.

Example: We purchased our house in mid-April. The sellers gave their receipt to the estate agent, who did the math so we could reimburse the sellers for the remaining eight and a half months of the year.

2. Registration of the Property

The property must be registered in your name at the *Registro de la Propiedad.*

This ensures:

- legal recognition of ownership
- protection against third-party claims

In practice:

- the notary usually sends the deed
- your lawyer or gestor completes the process

3. Updating the *Catastro*

The *Catastro* (cadastral register) must also reflect the new ownership.

This is used for:

- tax calculations (IBI)
- administrative records

This is usually handled automatically—but it is worth confirming that the update has been completed.

4. Transferring Utilities

You will need to transfer or set up:

- electricity
- water
- gas (if applicable)
- internet

What you typically need:

- copy of the deed
- ID/NIE/TIE
- bank account details

A practical tip:

Do this as early as possible to avoid service interruptions. Keep a time-stamped photo of the meter readings in case anyone wants to challenge your readings.

5. Informing the Community of Owners

If your property is part of a shared building:

- notify the *Comunidad de Propietarios*
- provide your contact details

This ensures:

- correct billing of fees
- communication about meetings and building works

6. Setting Up Insurance

You should arrange home insurance (*seguro de hogar*).

If you have a mortgage, insurance may be required by the bank. You will need to provide proof.

Even without a mortgage, insurance is strongly recommended to cover:

- damage
- liability
- unforeseen events

7. Ongoing Costs to Be Aware of

Ownership comes with recurring expenses.

Typical ongoing costs:

- IBI (annual property tax)
- community fees, if applicable
- utilities
- maintenance and repairs
- insurance

These costs can vary significantly depending on the property—and should be factored into your long-term planning.

8. Renovations and Improvements

If you plan to carry out work:

- check whether permits are required
- obtain approval where necessary

Unapproved work can:

- lead to fines
- create problems when selling later

9. Renting Out the Property

If you intend to rent the property:

- check local regulations
- confirm licensing requirements

In Catalonia:

Short-term rentals are:

- strictly regulated
- often restricted

Do not assume you can rent freely.

10. Keeping Documents Safe

You should keep copies of:

- the deed (*escritura*)
- tax payment confirmations
- utility contracts
- insurance policies

A practical tip:

Store both physical and digital copies. A fireproof box is advisable for the physical documents.

A Simple Way to Think About It

Buying the property is a transaction.
Owning it is an ongoing responsibility.

Common Oversights

After completion, buyers sometimes:

- delay transferring utilities
- overlook tax deadlines
- assume everything is handled automatically
- underestimate ongoing costs

In most cases, problems arise not from complexity—but from inattention.

A Practical Approach

To keep things simple:

- confirm what your lawyer is handling
- create a checklist of post-purchase tasks
- complete key steps within the first few weeks

The transition from buyer to owner is where the experience becomes real.

Handled well:

- the process feels smooth and complete

Handled poorly:

- small issues can become ongoing frustrations

Closing Thought

At this stage, the hardest part is behind you.

You have:

- navigated an unfamiliar system

- made informed decisions
- and completed the purchase

Now you can focus on making the property your own.

Conclusion
Moving Forward with Confidence

Buying property in Catalonia can feel complicated at first.

The process is different, the terminology unfamiliar, and the financial stakes high. It is entirely natural to feel uncertain—especially when you are dealing with a system that does not work in the same way as in your home country.

But as you have seen throughout this guide, the process itself is not unpredictable.

It follows a structure.
The key decisions are identifiable.
And most risks become manageable once they are properly understood.

Problems usually arise not because the system is designed to mislead, but because:

- assumptions are carried over from elsewhere
- important checks are skipped
- decisions are made under pressure

Preparation matters far more than luck.

If there is one idea at the heart of this book, it is this:

Understand the process before you commit yourself to it.

You do not need to become an expert in Spanish property law. But you do need enough understanding to:

- ask sensible questions
- recognize potential problems
- and make decisions deliberately rather than reactively

The professionals involved in the process—estate agents, lawyers, banks, and notaries—all play important roles. But none replaces your own understanding of what you are doing and why.

Buying a property is one of the most significant financial decisions most people will ever make. It is also often an emotional one, tied to ideas about lifestyle, security, and the future.

Clarity helps keep those emotions from becoming costly mistakes.

Whether you are still exploring, actively searching, or preparing to sign a purchase contract, you are now in a stronger position than when you began.

The process may be different—but with preparation and a clear understanding of how it works, it is entirely manageable.

Author's Note

This book is not written from the perspective of a lawyer, a real estate agent, or a financial institution.

It is written from the perspective of someone who has gone through the process of buying property in Catalonia—and who, at the time, would have benefited from a clear and practical guide.

Like many foreign buyers, I encountered a system that worked differently from what I was used to. The information available was often fragmented, overly technical, or assumed prior knowledge that I did not have.

What I needed was not more information, but better structure.

This book has been an attempt to provide that structure.

If it helps you avoid even one unnecessary complication, it has served its purpose.

Disclaimer: This book is intended as a practical guide and does not constitute legal or financial advice. For specific situations, professional advice should always be sought.

About the Author

Allen J. Woppert is a writer based in Catalonia. Born in the United States, he has spent most of his adult life in Germany and Spain. His experiences purchasing property in Catalonia inspired him to write this book.

A German-language edition of this guide is also available.

Updated resources, downloadable tables and checklists, as well as additional information are available at www.allenjwoppert.com.

> Certain Companion Resources are meant for people who purchased my books. They can be accessed at:
> allenjwoppert.com/rrreaderresources

www.ingramcontent.com/pod-product-compliance
Lightning Source LLC
Chambersburg PA
CBHW070645240926
51846CB00003BA/794
* 9 7 8 8 4 0 9 8 6 5 8 9 5 *